GW01085640

ROLF HARRIS

THE MOST TALENTED MAN IN THE WORLD

ROLF HARRIS

THE MOST
TALENTED MAN
IN THE WORLD

by Michael Heatley

Twisterella Books
London

Twisterella Books
P.O.Box 14691, London SE1 3ZJ

Published by Twisterella Books 1997

British Library Cataloguing-in-Publication Data
A catalogue for this book is available from The British Library

ISBN 1-901483-01-0

Printed and bound in Great Britain

Photo Credits in order of appearance: 1-3: Harry Goodwin; 4: Nick
Matthews/SIN; 5-8: Kim Tonelli/SIN; 9: Andrew Murray/All Action;
10: Doug Peters/All Action; 11: Kim Tonelli/SIN
Cover Photo by Tim Rooke/Rex Features

Cover designed by Phil Gambrill
Text designed by Twisterella Books

Many thanks to Nigel Cross for additional research

Dedicated to Kaye Roach

CONTENTS

INTRODUCTION

If you were to ask the average man or women in the street the name of the most famous Australian alive, their answer would unswervingly be Rolf Harris. Forget other popular figures from 'down under' like Kylie Minogue, Jason Donovan, or even Dame Edna Everage – it would be Rolf's name that rolled trippingly off their tongues! For more than 40 years, Rolf has been Australia's unofficial cultural ambassador – step aside Sir Les Patterson – who, armed with wit and humanity and, of course, his trusty didgeridoo, has done more for his country than any number of international Aussie lager advertising campaigns!

Described by *The Daily Telegraph*, no less, as 'a renaissance man', Rolf Harris is not only in possession of many talents but also many faces: an entertainer who has delighted generations of children with his humourous characterisations and zany live-in-the-studio paintings and cartoons; a comedian who, though now well into his seventh decade, enjoys a big cult following on the college circuit; a novelist; a photographer whose *Rolf Harris Picture Show* has been exhibited by Kodak both in Britain and abroad and whose work has also been shown to the Royal Photographic Society; and last, but far from least, a singer and musician who not only shared the stage with the Beatles but also their producer.

With his calling cards – the ubiquitous specs and beard, plus his wobble board and pot of paint always at the ready – Rolf continues to this day to confound the cynics and enjoy wave after wave of success, just when even he thought it might finally be time to bow out gracefully. He has, after all, broken one of show business's most sacred rules – never work with children and animals – to carve himself out an exalted niche in the pantheon of the entertainment world. He's a chap who readily admits to being no genius but who always seems to have the uncanny knack of plucking victory from the jaws of defeat. His success, he told *Radio Times*, lies in the way he approaches life. 'I like to talk to everyone and be accessible…what I try to do is simple – spread a little love and affection whenever I have the chance.'

In May 1997 Rolf was awarded Life Membership of the RSPCA for his committed work to three series of BBC TV's hugely popular *Animal Hospital*. It seemed entirely appropriate that a celebrity who'd first shot to prominence with a hit single about a kangaroo some 37 years before, should end up being honoured by an organisation known for its reputation worldwide as the best in animal welfare! For Rolf it was just one more example of his positive attitude to life paying dividends of a kind that far outweighs fame and wealth.

CHAPTER 1: SUN ARISE

Rolf Harris was born on 30 March 1930 in Bassendean, Perth, Western Australia. His father, Cromwell Harris had emigrated to the Antipodes and taken up sheep farming there with his brother. He left the love of his life, Marjory, back home in Cardiff and proposed to her by letter – she subsequently joined him and they were married out there. They became a family when their first child, Bruce, came along – he'd later become Rolf's manager.

Being an Aries, Rolf has always been a man of strong passions and, from a very early age, showed a love for water and swimming. The Swan River gurgled past their house and, at the tender age of four, he fell in. He couldn't swim and it looked like he might drown, but he somehow managed to doggie-paddle his way back to the bank. When he told his mum of this feat, she was incensed and subsequently had him take swimming lessons at Crawley Baths in Perth, but it was an incident that graphically stayed with him. Indeed, many years later, he'd actually recall the experience in a famous nationwide water safety advert he did for British television!

His early years were like those of many other kids growing up immediately before and during World

War II. Rolf's childhood passed without major incident – though at the age of six he was debilitated by a serious bout of scarlet fever, from which it took him a long time to fully recover. Looking back on it in 1993, he told the *Midland News Association* 'I had a magical childhood. I never wanted to leave childhood, I loved it so much – so I decided not to. When you get to be an adult, if you're lucky you remember what it was like to be a child. I think most adults never remember, but I do and I remember the adults I liked as a child.'

His mother was keen on amateur dramatics and was regularly out of the house rehearsing – and it was because of this that Rolf had his first lesson in self-sufficiency. He learned to cook. 'The one thing I can cook is the best scrambled eggs you've ever seen,' he'd later tell *Somerfield Magazine*. 'My mum taught me when I was a kid...she'd be off rehearsing quite often – knowing that if I was starving I could fix myself scrambled eggs in case she was ever late!'

He attended Bassendean School and later Perth Modern High, where his main interests were music – he made his public debut at 11 – art and swimming, a sport at which he soon began to excel. When he was 15, he won the Junior Backstroke Championship of Australia in Melbourne. 'Winning that championship was a thrill I'll never forget,' he'd later reminisce fondly. 'Maybe I was a bit of a swimmer because as a kid I was constantly thrown into the river at the bottom of our garden by my elder brother Bruce, usually for being cheeky!' Sadly his prospects as a champion swimmer were eventually to come to nothing as he told *Radio Times*, 'I was a very good swimmer but when I was 21 I picked up some bug in the river and by the time I got home I couldn't move my head, shoulders or legs. I thought I had polio and was resigned to being immobile for the rest of my life. I was fatalistic, not cross or angry. What can you do? Slowly I got better...'

On finishing secondary school, it seemed as if his future might lie in education. To that end, he took a teacher-training course at the University of Western Australia and taught at a local school in Perth. There's little doubt the skills he picked up then have stood him in good stead in the career he ended up following. But no one job was wide-reaching enough to let him display his many talents, and at the same time as teaching he was also doing painting, sketches and playing the piano. This last skill won him a number of local talent contests, and in 1949, aged 18, Rolf won the legendary *Amateur Hour* competition on Australian radio.

However, his main burgeoning passion was painting – his grandfather had been a Welsh portrait painter so it obviously ran in the family genes! It was soon to bring him to a momentous decision, and it was one he was to face up to during the period of recuperation after contracting the meningitis bug from the river that nearly proved so catastrophic. 'While I was lying there I realised teaching wasn't for me', he recalled in *Radio Times*, 'I wanted to pursue my art and find out how far I could go.'

In 1952, while thousands of British families were emigrating to the land of sun and opportunity, 22-year-old Rolf Harris resolved to go the other way and sailed to the UK to study art. He arrived in London with his life savings, just £297, in his pocket and enrolled at art college. To make ends meet, he started to dabble as an entertainer, and got his first break on the stage in *One Under Eight*, 'I was lucky to have so many strings to my bow...music, singing, drawing.' One of his first jobs was to appear at the Down Under Club in west London's Earl's Court - a ghetto for homesick Australians. His residency at the club was to last six years on and off and he honed an act as a stand-up comic and singer.

It wasn't an instant success, but his confidence grew and he began to make a name for himself. The restaurants of Earls Court offered Rolf his first taste of Indian cuisine, something for which he's since developed a self-confessed addiction. 'I got hooked on curries when I first came to London. Now I get withdrawal symptoms if I don't have one once a week – my mouth starts to water just hearing the word. My wife does a *wonderful* curry.'

Rolf's red-hot talents then came to the attention of the BBC, whose Children's Department had launched its first ever magazine programme, *Whirligig*, in November 1950. Presented by Humphrey Lestocq, the show also featured the popular Steve Race at the piano and a puppet named Mr Turnip. Rolf wrote for an audition simply because he'd seen someone doing drawings on television when he'd been round at the house of a family whose two little children got up and went outside to play. 'That mirrored my feelings exactly,' said Rolf. 'I thought if I couldn't do better than that guy I'd want my bloody head examined.' It wasn't anything to do with the drawings, which were superb, but the fact that each drawing started exactly the same way as the previous one had. They also took an age to complete. Rolf, who had something rather more instant and entertaining in mind, joined *Jigsaw* – as the programme had now become known – to spin yarns and illustrate the exploits of a puppet called Fuzz. It was to prove an effective training ground for what was to come.

Meanwhile his talent as an artist was blossoming and his paintings were exhibited at the Royal Academy of Art in London in 1956. It was during his time at art school that he met his wife-to-be, sculptress and jewellery-designer Alwen Hughes, and they were married on 1 March 1958. Oddly enough, their bridesmaid on the great day was none other than Pugsy, Alwen's pet poodle and the incident was to prove the first of many illustrating the couple's obsessive, even eccentric love of animals. Alwen, who claims she was 'an eccentric child', said the dog's recruitment 'saved a lot of problems', while Rolf later elaborated that his wife's idea had successfully avoided any family problems. 'I don't know if there would have been squabbles about who should be the bridesmaids, but they were nipped in the bud.'

The couple's beloved daughter Bindi was born on 10 March 1964. 'Bindi Bindi is an Aboriginal name of a place in Western Australia which we quite liked,' Rolf later explained when asked the origin of her name. 'Don't ask me what it means though.' She was to be their only child – as Rolf later opined, 'I've always had driving ambition, which is one reason why I'm not sure I'd have liked more children. You wonder if your lifestyle would leave enough time to devote to them. Careers are very destructive of relationships among families.'

During his tenure at the Down Under Club, Rolf wrote what was to become his first big hit single, 'Tie Me Kangaroo Down Sport', in 1957 and subsequently performed it every week there for the homesick Antipodeans who gathered to watch. 'I wrote this song for them so it would have a chorus they could all sing,' he said. Two years later the Harrises returned to the land of Oz when Rolf was invited to compere and produce a kids' TV show – and, while there, he took the opportunity to record the first version of the song at a studio in Perth. 'It was the time that calypsos were the rage,' he'd later say, 'and I thought I'd write a (Harry) Belafonte-type Australian song to amuse the club members. I tried to bring in everything Australian I could think of, as many animal Australian slang terms and nicknames as possible – and gradually got an original tune with about 18 verses.' His brother Bruce gave him considerable help with the beginning and the joke ending of the song.

When released domestically, 'Kangaroo' became an instant hit, going to Number 1 and staying there for several weeks, earning him a gold disc in the process. The single was released in the UK to similar popularity on EMI's Columbia label (home to such happening popsters as Cliff Richard and the Shadows) and climbed up to the Number 9 position. In 1962 Rolf would re-record the song with George Martin who would act as the Antipodean's producer on and off for much of the next decade, but who as everyone knows found fame and fortune as the man who produced the Beatles' staggering run of hits in the 1960s.

Rolf would observe in the liner notes to a 1994 EMI compilation, *Didgereely-Doo All That: The Best*

Of Rolf Harris, 'In later years I removed one verse, which had given some offence and actually caused the song to be banned in Singapore (thereby increasing record sales enormously!).' The single enjoyed equal acclaim in Canada and in the USA where it was a bit of a sleeper, eventually hitting the *Billboard* chart in June 1963. But though it reached Number 3, it was to prove his only real American success and left him with a reputation as something of a one-hit wonder over there (though he enjoyed a good career as a club entertainer).

The B-side 'Nick Teen And Al K Hall' was equally humourous – it was inspired by a radio programme Rolf had heard in the early 1950s which featured a roving Aussie reporter, Wilf Thomas, and had been broadcast from somewhere in South America. The Latino music featured on it had prompted him to write something in similar vein.

All of a sudden out of the blue, this enthusiastic four-eyed, moustachioed wielder of the paintbrush was an international pop star – albeit a reluctant one, as he later observed in *Radio Times*: 'I only started singing when I was 30 – too old – and I missed the first flush of "couldn't-care-less" 18-year-olds. When "Rock Around The Clock" came out with Bill Haley in the 1950s, I was playing piano-accordion, which wasn't really a rock 'n' roll instrument. I felt you had to play guitar and have a broad American accent. I made a strong commitment to myself not to do that.

'It's stupid to be phoney and pretend you're someone else – like so many Australians have done over the years. They cancel the accent and put on this really heavy American one to gain success, not realising the shattering truth that there are a million real Yanks.'

The amazing international success of 'Kangaroo' brought Rolf back to the UK. It was a fantastic time to be in the English capital city, post-war austerity was at an end, while 'Swinging London' and the equally swinging 1960s were just about to break. He returned via live appearances in the States and Canada including a visit to the West Coast city of Vancouver, about which he'd later confess, 'the city and I have had a sort of mutual love affair since 1961.'

Rolf's follow-up single for Columbia, 'Tame Eagle' b/w 'Uncomfortable Yogi' was something of a flop, but he had another tune up his sleeve that would soon return him to the charts. Released in October 1962, 'Sun Arise' featured an Aboriginal wind instrument called the didgeridoo...and turned it into a household word almost overnight! The song was based on an authentic native Australian chant, as Rolf explained in his *Best Of* album liner notes.

'This was written in 1960 after Harry Butler played me tapes of the first Australian Aboriginal singing I'd ever heard. The didgeridoo accompaniment fascinated me and I recorded an authentic-sounding version that year with Professor Trevor Jones playing didgeridoo. It sold very badly. Back in England in '62, I played that recording to George Martin, who said it was boring. My hackles went up, "It's authentic," I said. "That's the way they sing, over and over on the same phrase." George said, "I love the sound of it, but it really is boring. See if you can create a middle bit, which still has that authentic feel, then when you come back to the repetitive bit, you know it and it's like an old friend."

'That's what happened. With a middle bit and an end bit written, Johnny Spence created the arrangement using eight bass fiddles to simulate a didgeridoo sound (I couldn't play the didgeridoo at that time, and knew no-one in England who could). George insisted that EMI kept plugging the song for three months, and suddenly the public got used to the weird new sound and it went to Number 3. I was sure it was going to be Number 1, but the following week, some fellow called Elvis Presley jumped right into that spot from nowhere and spoiled my chances.' Nonetheless it stayed in the UK charts for 16 weeks.

Thirty years and more later, the didgeridoo is regarded as one of the instruments responsible for popularising world music: indeed, it's not uncommon to see dreadlocked youths playing them on the street corners of British cities, while top bands like the Levellers and the aptly named Dr Didg have featured the instrument heavily in their own music.

So is Rolf the godfather of world music, the man who practically single-handedly invented the genre? 'Well, I don't know about that,' he told *Q* in 1993, 'I suppose in a way I did. I pioneered world music, certainly. You see, I've been fascinated by the didgeridoo from the time I first heard it. I just find it a most haunting and primitive, primal thing which seems to go through your gut. It's a very safe, secure thing which all primitive people have...the Tibetans stand in a circle and do that powerful humming thing which becomes a trance-inducing thing...they go off into another world and it's wonderful.'

The flipside, which rejoiced in the saucy title of 'Someone's Pinched Me Winkles', was in fact an ode to the winklepicker shoe. And thereby hung a tale, as an unusually annoyed Rolf revealed to *Q*. It turned out to have been inspired by the barrel-like, pasty-faced British comedian Charlie Drake who enjoyed similar novelty hits during the same era as Rolf: things like 'Please Mr Custer I Don't Want To Go'.

'I wrote that as a result of Charlie Drake having a big hit with "My Boomerang Won't Come Back". I was outraged that he should mock the Aborigines to such an extent, with so many bloody false bits of information in that bloody song. I got really uptight about that, so I went and wrote a Cockney song with as many bloody false bits of information in it as I could as a sort of protest.'

Hit records meant that Rolf would rub shoulders with many of the period's pop stars and he recalled some of his amazing experiences in *Q*: 'I was on a Larry Parnes tour with Joe Brown and the Bruvvers and Eden Kane...and the Tornados with Clem Cattini on drums and Heinz...and there was that bloke who changed his name to Alvin Stardust. What was his name? Shane Fenton? His real name was Bernard Jewry. And so Shane was on it and I travelled with him all the time.

'He had this big driver, Eddie Falcon, and I'd never seen violence before, because my dad was the most pacifist guy, so when I did see violence I was appalled. We'd come into a town and all the local boys would be up in arms against all these pop stars because all the local girls would flocking around them and this guy Eddie Falcon used to travel with an iron bar down his coat sleeve and if there was any trouble, that bar would come out, I can bloody tell you. I was appalled!

'But I did have one funny experience on that tour because we were doing a bloody dance hall in Epsom and I did my spot and I came off stage absolutely disgusted! And I said to the promoter, Never again! There were young kids out there drunk! Youngsters of 12 years old drunk out of their heads and they were smoking cigars. This is absolutely disgusting. And the promoter said to me, What do you mean, young kids? They're jockeys! Cor, what a shock *that* was!'

During 'Sun Arise's chart run in late 1962, another George Martin-produced record entered the Top 30. It was 'Love Me Do', the first of many hits by four mop-topped Liverpudlians, and it was somehow inevitable that Rolf's path would cross with those of the Beatles. They'd share the billing on many shows together, the first of which took place on 18 April 1963 when they appeared at the Royal Albert Hall with a cast that also included George Melly, Del Shannon, Lance Percival and the Springfields. The show – snappily titled *Swinging Sound 63* – was broadcast live by the BBC, and Rolf was subsequently hired by the Beeb to interview the Fab Four. Knowing full well that Lennon and company were already veterans at taking the Michael out of media presenters, he broke the ice by venturing, 'Ringo, what do you think of spaghetti?' It worked perfectly.

He'd later join them for more shows, including one broadcast by the BBC which culminated in the quartet backing Harris on an impromptu but nonetheless rocking version of 'Tie Me Kangaroo

Down Sport' – complete with Beatle harmonies that boasted new lyrics about their haircuts and names! In the current era of the Beatles hugely-successful *Anthology* series, somebody really ought to scour the vaults of Broadcasting House for this little gem!

With this entertaining track record in mind, Rolf was an obvious choice to act as Master of Ceremonies for the Beatles' Christmas Shows at London's Finsbury Park Astoria (later to become noted rock venue the Rainbow) that ran from 24 December 1963 to 11 January 1964. The shows were more than just pop concerts: they were feasts of family entertainment conceived and produced by Beatles' manager Brian Epstein and incorporated elements of pantomime, music and comedy.

It must have been quite a punishing schedule, a 16-night run with two shows per night except 24 and 31 December and no performances at all on 25 and 29 December and 5 January. By then, Beatlemania was sweeping the nation and the lovable lads had a brace of hit records under their belts. The tickets – all 100,000 of them – went on sale on 21 October 1963 and were sold out by 16 November, mainly bought up by their rabid female teenage fans.

They may not have been there to see him, but the whole intensity of the experience clearly left its mark on the amiable Australian. 'Compering that show was amazing,' Rolf recalled fully three decades later. As a fellow musician, he was disappointed the crowd didn't give the Beatles a fair hearing and attempted to put the point across...inevitably, to little avail. 'I used to tell the kids, "last night no one could hear a thing because of all your screaming. Now *listen to the music.* Ladies and Gentlemen, the Beatles!". The music, and the noise, was amazing!'

Far from being grateful, a mischievous John Lennon and Paul McCartney tried to sabotage his own set one night by breaking into one of his songs with an off-stage microphone. Rolf was not amused, and afterwards took them to task for lack of professionalism! 'I got more respect from that point but less friendship,' he later commented. Rolf also drew a cartoon of the group as a souvenir of the shows: they liked it so much it was later reprinted and sent out to members of the Beatles' UK fan club.

His adventures with the world-beating Scousers may have been a mixed bag but his next single seemed to affirm that he still thought of them as top of the pops. 'Ringo For President' (b/w 'Headhunter') caught the raging Beatle-mad mood of the nation better than most of the novelty records that came in their wake – things like Dora Bryan's 'All I Want For Christmas Is A Beatle'. In the meanwhile, though, 'Johnny Day', the official follow-up to 'Sun Arise', had failed to set the charts on fire, peaking at Number 44 in 1963.

Years later, on 3 April 1969, Rolf shared one more bill with a Beatle – but under very different circumstances. This time he was appearing on *The Eamonn Andrews Show* live from the restaurant of the Cafe Royal in London's Regent Street with a line up that featured Jack Benny, Gaynor Jones, Yehudi Menuhin, and John Lennon and Yoko Ono. The pair were then at the height of their serious peace campaign and bed-ins and totally vilified by the media.

One couldn't help but think that – in the uncomfortable atmosphere of the general discussion segment of the show, as John espoused his heartfelt, new-found philosophies and politics – those crazy innocent fun-filled times Harris and Lennon had shared six years before now seemed centuries away. Rolf had, perhaps, more in common with the other member of the Fabs' hit songwriting duo: years later, he would respectfully comment, 'Paul McCartney. You look at that guy and you say he's done it right.'

His experiences with the Beatles may have been fleeting but, by the mid 1960s, Rolf Harris had established himself as one of the world's top entertainers and recording artists. In Britain he was now big business and, even though he'd see no more chart action for a couple of years or so, Harris was still recording and was now in big demand for television work. As a live performer, too, he'd appear at the *Talk Of The Town* and on the prestigious *Royal Variety Performance*.

CHAPTER 2: TWO LITTLE BOYS

By the summer of 1966 Rolf was fronting one of the most popular kids' shows on TV that ran neck and neck in the viewing stakes with such flagship productions as *Crackerjack*. Usually broadcast late on Friday afternoons, *Hey Presto, It's Rolf* was an action-packed 40 minutes of songs, sketches, audience participation and appearances of top pop bands of the day. The added ingredient was, of course, Rolf, paint pot and brush in hand rattling off quickie paintings on a gigantic canvas or, marker pen at the ready, zipping off one of his ingenious cartoons with his trademark phrase, 'can you tell what it is yet?'

This infamous catchphrase would eventually go down in legend, and comedians like the rubber-faced Phil Cool would later use it as part of their impersonations of the great man. 'It's marvellous – wonderful,' Rolf later told the *Midland News Association*. 'At least they know who you are. Actually, we're great friends of Phil's – he's incredible.'

But perhaps the most lasting legacy of this TV series were some of the characters and songs that were featured in it. Diminutive Seamus O'Sean the Leprechaun made regular appearances alongside the equally delightful Coojee Bear, based on that cute and now endangered Australian marsupial the koala. Coojee Bear would later be honoured by a 50-minute cartoon adventure film, *Coojee Bear And The Monster*. Masterminded by Rolf's musical director Barry Booth, this incorporated narration, songs and music performed by a symphony orchestra along with no fewer than 400 on-screen illustrations.

The film was premiered in June 1982 in Knoxville, Tennessee at the Expo '82 where Rolf was doing his bit for his country (he's currently represented Australia at a total of six world fairs). And *Coojee Bear* would also have its soundtrack of memorable tunes like 'Sean The Shoemaker' and 'Vroom, Vroom, Vroom' subsequently released as an album by Solid Records.

But perhaps the most famous creation was Jake the Peg, a character from one of Rolf's most enduring songs that still features in his live set today. Talking about it in the notes to *Didgereely-Doo All That*, Rolf recalled, 'In the mid-1960s I did a lot of work in Vancouver in Canada. On one of these trips, I was booked as the only professional in a predominantly amateur Lion's Club concert. While I was waiting to go on, the man out on the stage, working in front of a "front cloth", was getting enormous laughs – so much so that when I started, they were still chuckling about his performance ten minutes into my act!

'I found out afterwards that the fellow was Frank Roosen, a Dutchman, and that he'd been singing a song about a man with three legs. I got in contact with him, and he was thrilled that I should be interested in his song. It was the only thing he'd ever written. When he sang it to me, I felt the end petered out, and asked him if he'd be happy if I did some work on trying to get a rounded ending. He agreed, so I took his song back to England, got his air mail approval for my additional bits and the new last verse, and recorded it at Abbey Road. The accent I'm putting on is my attempt to copy Frank's infectious Dutch-sounding English.'

The cricketing joke in the lyrics has always gone down well with his cork and willow-mad fellow countryman, and the sight of Rolf wiggling about up onstage with the third leg concealed under his raincoat has always been a showstopper with audiences past and present.

In the mid 1960s Rolf enjoyed many radio hits especially with some of the children's tunes he recorded that were some of the most requested on the BBC's Light Programme (later Radio 1)'s *Children's Favourites* presented by Uncle Mac and later Ed 'Stewpot' Stewart. Among these was the memorable 'I've Lost My Mummy', which George Martin produced. Rolf observed that the song, which he wrote himself, was based on his own childhood experience of being lost in a big shop.

The song was first recorded in Australia without an audience, and just didn't work. Re-recorded in front of an audience in Abbey Road studios with Laurie Holloway directing the audience, it worked – and how! 'I remember,' said Rolf, 'when I did the first noisy intake of breath and belted out, "I've lost my mummy", one man in the audience laughed so hard, that he went scarlet in the face and actually fell off his chair.'

Equally popular was 'Court Of King Caractacus', another George Martin-produced masterpiece which was recorded in New York. Rolf had found the song in a boy scout's campfire songbook and liked it so much, he greatly expanded the original three verses with three more cumulative verses, each getting longer as the song proceeded in the vein of 'I Know An Old Lady Who Swallowed A Fly.'

In the 1980s, Rolf was contacted by an American attorney who sent a tape of a song from an old 78rpm record entitled 'The King Of Caractacus'. The lawyer was acting on behalf of the daughter of the man who'd originally written it. Rolf's original source had credited the song as 'traditional' but, ever the good guy, he went back over the accounts and charitably paid out half the royalties the recording had made him.

In 1967 Rolf made his bid for the prime-time TV slot with the first of a continuing series of early

Saturday evening shows. BBC 1 broadcast the first series of *The Rolf Harris Show* from January through March 1967 and it became as integral part of Saturday-night entertainment as *The Avengers* and *Match Of The Day*. There was the usual mix of songs, sketches and cartoons, while popular dance troupe the New Generation, choreographed by Dougie Squire, pioneered a new kind of dancing which inspired a wave of groups such as Pan's People and, later, Hot Gossip!

The first series reached a triumphant climax on 11 March when, in front of 6.4 million viewers on a bill that included the Nitwits, Raphael and the Sadri Dancers, a young bare-footed Sandie Shaw performed the entries for *A Song For Europe*. Four weeks later, Rolf would introduce the *Eurovision Song Contest* from the Hofburg, Vienna where Sandie's 'Puppet On A String' was the winning entry for the UK.

The series ran again in the early months of both 1968 and 1969, reaching a peak of 7.2 million viewers. Among the featured guests were the Dudley Moore Trio, Dusty Springfield and a young American singer-songwriter named Janis Ian, who'd find fame with 'At Seventeen'. One of the most intriguing elements of the shows was that, in addition to the now-famous didgeridoo and wobble board, Rolf had 'discovered' a new instrument – a small hand-held keyboard called 'the Stylophone'.

Talking in *Q* many years later, Rolf recalled the little organ with a mixture of amusement and irritation. 'This guy invented the machine and brought it to my show's producer and said, I've got this great new electronic organ. It was the first of its kind. It was the forerunner of all the synthesizers and bloody keyboard things and we used it quite a bit on the show...actually the stylophone didn't have a very pleasing sound. It was likened by some bloke to a demented bee trapped in a bloody bottle!'

Whatever his feelings Rolf enjoyed a long association with the instrument, doing product endorsement and even producing a book, published by EMI in 1974 – *Standards And Classics For The Rolf Harris Stylophone*. Yet although Rolf should by rights have been credited for its 'discovery' in the same way as he'd popularised the didgeridoo – sadly that privilege fell to a young musician who lived close to Rolf in South London, David Bowie. In the autumn of 1969, after years of struggling, Bowie enjoyed his first major hit – in the wake of man's first triumphant walk on the moon, 'Space Oddity' cracked the Top 10 and in the song's instrumental break, the stylophone could be heard whooshing through the galaxy like a burning meteorite.

Rolf could have been forgiven for being piqued,

since by then it looked as if his own chart-topping days were well and truly over. He had to take comfort in accepting other kinds of prestigious honours such as in 1968, when he was awarded an MBE. But he still continued to write songs and record them – indeed, in 1967 he was commissioned to write some material to promote a new round-the-world route pioneered by British Overseas Airways Corporation (the forerunner of today's British Airways). This was later issued as an EP record given away to publicise the service.

One of the songs, 'Fijian Girl', was to enjoy a rather longer life, yet hadn't remotely been inspired by the tropical island of the title. The first part of the tune was inspired by a Russian choir recording he'd heard. The song was going to be all about Hawaii, a stop on the new route. The reason it was changed to Fiji was that he met an Australian school teacher while doing cabaret in Vancouver who'd been working in Fiji and was able to give Rolf lots of background material.

In April 1969, Columbia released a new single, 'Bluer Than Blue', which grazed the Top 30 and then fell rapidly from sight. Musical tastes were changing: the kids who'd loved 'Jake The Peg' a few years previously had grown up, grown their hair and were listening to more serious, heavier sounds. It was the end of the 1960s, a time of great political and social upheaval. Society's boundaries were being re-drawn between the establishment and the rainbow-hued aspirations of a new generation demanding a better world. Sincere as it may have been, 'Bluer Than Blue' was seen almost as a joke when set against some of the other contenders in the chart in that month – classic songs such as Jethro Tull's 'Living In The Past', The Who's 'Pinball Wizard' and the Beatles 'Get Back'.

However it was during that period that Rolf came across a tune that was to launch him to new heights of fame and popularity. With a third series of his television series safely under his belt, Rolf had taken his family on a much-needed holiday to Arnhem Land in Northern Australia. Their love of the unspoilt landscape and aboriginal way of life lead them to meet Ted Egan, Administrator for Aboriginal Affairs in Darwin, and the Harris family stayed with him at his home in the tiny habitation of Gove.

'One morning,' Rolf later recalled in the *Didgereely-Doo All That?* notes, 'he said, "This'd be great for your television show in England", and he proceeded to beat out a rhythm on the table and sing me this song that I thought was really namby pamby and awful. You can imagine those first couple of lines being sung in a gentle tenor voice, "Two little boys had two little toys".

'I was sitting there, feeling quite uncomfortable, and wondering what I was going to say to him about the song when he'd finished because he was such a nice bloke, and it was such an awful song. Suddenly he was singing the line, "do you think I would leave you dying?" and all the hair stood up on the back of my neck and on my arms. It really grabbed me from that moment, and turned my opinion of the song right around. I got out my reel to reel tape recorder and got him to sing it again while I recorded it.'

When Rolf arrived back in the UK, he enthusiastically discussed the idea of using the song on the TV with producer Stuart Morris – but, tragedy of tragedies, he had somehow managed to lose the tape on his travels. There was only one thing for it but to call up Ted thousands of miles away and have him sing it again down the phone! His friend's dulcet tones duly committed to tape, albeit from several thousand miles' distance, Rolf set about recording it.

The song had been written in 1903 about two childhood friends, Joe and Jack, who'd been separated by the American Civil War and who were reunited in adult life on a battlefield where Jack, remembering an incident from their early years, saves his pal's life. Alan Braden dreamed up the 'Victorian' feel to the song's arrangement, and the tune went down a storm when Rolf performed before an audience in the TV studio. He then went into the recording studio to cut it as a single, and this was where the song underwent further significant changes. As Rolf recalled, 'on take three we did a dramatic slowing down during the uniform drum roll in the middle, so that no-one was aware of the tempo change until the words failed to come in again when you expected them to at the end of the drum roll.

'That tempo change made all the difference. At the end of the session, we had one spare track, so I asked Freddy Clayton, one of the trumpeters, if he'd re-record his trumpet call at the end without listening to his previous recording. In this way, he'd hear all the other tracks, and would maybe be slightly out of phase with himself to give a ghostly 'empty parade ground' effect. It worked perfectly.'

In 1969 Peter Green's Fleetwood Mac were the most popular pop act in Great Britain, their record sales that year outstripping those of both the Beatles and the Rolling Stones – but it was Rolf Harris who saw out the decade with his record at the top of the UK chart. Released on 22 November, 'Two Little Boys' shot to pole position and remained there for a staggering six weeks, going on to sell over a million copies. Interestingly enough, it was Rolf's only hit not to have an Aussie theme. The quintessential Christmas record, it became both the last Number 1 of the 1960s and the first of the 1970s, enjoying the dubious privilege of being the longest-running chart-topper since Engelbert

Humperdinck's 'Last Waltz' in autumn 1967.

Seen as nothing more than a joke by the longhairs, the single's appeal was nonetheless universal. Said Rolf years later in *Q*: 'Little kids loved the story and sort of quietened down when they heard it. And women loved it because it made them cry and made them emotional. And men liked it because it was a good marching tune and it said a lot about companionship and comradeship between blokes. It's a marvellous yarn... Much later, my auntie said to me that "Two Little Boys" was the story of my father and his brother, my uncle Carl in the First World War...'

Generous to a fault, Rolf assigned some of the song's royalties to Ted Egan – 'My accountant was horrified with what I did with the money from "Two Little Boys",' he told *The Sun* in 1993. 'I gave ten per cent to the guy who sang me the song in the first instance. Everybody thought I was mad, but without him I'd never have heard the song. I also gave a percentage to the guy who did the orchestration. My accountant was horrified. He told me I was mad. Nobody else does that.'

CHAPTER 3: ROLF RULES OK

Undoubtedly assisted by the the success of 'Two Little Boys', Rolf was voted TV Personality of the Year by the Radio Industries Club in 1970 and was now recognised as a top-drawer entertainer throughout the world. But at the same time the hits really did begin to dry up – only a swift re-entry by his big hit, when it reached the Number 50 spot for one week in June 1970, troubled the chart compilers this decade.

But, as the man himself professes, he has many strings to his bow. So he put aside his musical ambitions and simply concentrated on being a celebrity and all-round entertainer. His popular Saturday evening programme moved over from the Beeb to ITV for a series between 1972 and 1974, still capable of drawing over six million viewers on a good week. Rolf became an integral part of that comfy world of pantomimes and summer seasons, mums and dads, aunties and grannies and little kids, but of little interest to teenagers and young adults. And releasing singles like 'Happy Birthday Father Christmas' b/w 'McAdam', one of his last for EMI, did nothing to change this image.

As jolly and seasonal as it was, 'Happy Birthday' failed to set the Christmas charts alight when it was released in late 1975. On television he'd perform songs like 'Jindabyne', which while boasting a pretty arrangement by Barry Booth and interesting lyrics – it was based on a poem by fellow Aussie Barbara Speight who'd been inspired to write it after a frightening experience she'd had lost in the snows up in the skiing country of New South Wales – curried no favour with a generation cutting its teeth on Bolan, Bowie and Roxy Music.

Also Rolf's something of an abstainer when it comes to smoking and drinking – 'but not because I'm a wowser', he quipped to *Night And Day*: A wowser? 'It's Australian, someone who doesn't do something and tries to stop everyone else from doing it.' Even during the heyday of the Swinging 1960s, he'd never been tempted to indulge in any drug-taking and later admitted that he'd lost his temper with one of his band members for smoking dope because 'marijuana doesn't seem to fit in with my image at all.'

However he could be more even-handed when he had to work with session musicians who as he put it 'smoked "grass" or snorted things up their nose.' When he was cutting a tune called 'Yarrabangee' in 1976 for instance, he recalled, 'I sort of stood back nervously aloof from it all for a while, but then we got into the session and I was playing didgeridoo and appreciating the musicianship from the others...I just stopped making judgements and enjoyed the sounds we were making.'

One of Rolf's most successful ventures during the 1970s was into the world of TV commercials. That generation of fans will never forget the aforementioned British water safety advert, the making of which was no laughing matter as he recalled in *Q*: 'I nearly got drowned making that bloody commercial because all the kids were mucking around and crawling all over me and they had me underwater and were holding me down. All of a sudden, I thought I'm going to drown me bloody self so I'm going to have to thump one of these kids. I'm actually going to have to whack them really bloody hard. Scared the shit out of me!' Another advert that was rather more fun to make was one he did for Cadbury's Buttons where he scoffed the chocs off his fingers while using a singing technique he referred to as 'eefing and eyefing'. He'd already employed this vocal sound to great effect on a tune he'd recorded back in the 1960s called 'Big Dog.'

He'd been introduced to the technique while working at the Blue Angel in New York in the mid 1960s by a man called Bobby Morgan who worked for Epic Records. 'I just loved this Tennessee country sound at first hearing, and seemed to be able to do it perfectly right away.' When he got back to Britain, he was driving to Shepherds Bush one day to rehearse his BBC television show when to relieve the boredom of being stuck in a traffic jam he started eefing away. 'I thought how much it sounded like a dog panting, so I grabbed a bit of paper and in about half a mile stretch of bumper creeping along the South Circular heading for Clapham I had written the song.' To cap it all, the song was recorded in one take...

In Australia, viewers would remember an ad Rolf did regularly for about ten years which rather fittingly sung the praises of a brand of paint called Taubam. There would be Rolf tapping out a rhythm on the lid of paint while singing 'trust British paints, sure can.' Indeed, it was while on the set in Sydney filming one of these paint commercials that the idea for the aforementioned 'Yarrabangee' first came to him. 'One of the crew,' he recalled, 'a feller known to all as "Big Al", had a pet word. Anything he couldn't remember the name for was called a "Yarrabangee". It was "where's the Yarrabangee tape?" "No worries mate, it's over there on the Yarrabangee". It became a buzz word of that long videotaping session.

'On the way back to England in the plane, I wrote the whole song, using the names of everyone in the close-knit, happy crew...all the way throughout the creative process, I guess I sort of imagined that, in my case, "Yarrabangee" was another word for a didgeridoo.' Indeed, such was Rolf's prowess at penning a quick pop ditty that in 1973 he even had a book published, *Write Your Own Pop Song With*

Rolf Harris that gave budding young tunesmiths some handy tips!

In his home country Rolf had, by now, become something of a national institution – in the winter of 1972, for example, he returned to Australia to film three hour-long specials which critically examined the current state of the nation and what it was like to be Australian. In September 1973 he took centre stage in a light entertainment show, the first to be staged in the architectural splendour of the brand new Opera House overlooking Sydney Harbour, and in 1975 he returned there to appear in a benefit concert for victims of the Darwin cyclone disaster.

The destruction of this city by Cyclone Tracey at Christmas 1974 particularly affected the singer as some close friends of his, the Leonard family, were caught up in the tragedy. Families were separated in a Blitz-style evacuation of the stricken town as kids and women folk were temporarily billeted with kind-hearted citizens in cities down in the south, while husbands and single men stayed behind to assist in the clearing-up and rebuilding. The effect on Rolf was for him to write one of his most emotional songs, 'Northern Territory', a sensitive and emotive ballad with some subtle guitar playing by Bab Gill.

He recalled the background to the song in the *Didgereely Do All That?* liner note. 'By sheer chance

I was on a television weeks later, in Melbourne and Colleen Leonard happened to be watching from the foster home where they were staying. She rang the TV station and got through to me, I jumped in a cab and three quarters of an hour later was sitting in the lounge where their sleeping bags were spread all over the floor, having a very emotional and happy reunion.

'Of course Colleen's husband Clive was slogging away with the other menfolk up in Darwin, but this song is virtually word for word what Colleen told me that night about their experience and their feelings and their aching desire to get back to their home. It was a long, supercharged, very emotional evening with some very dear friends.' Undoubtedly when the song came out in 1976, the heart-tugging, resonant final chorus of 'No, I can't wait to get back home to Darwin' must have brought back some powerful memories for all the victims concerned.

Rolf wasn't just a hero on two continents...he was enjoying huge popularity in North America, too! He represented Australia at the 1974 Expo in Spokane, Washington, and regularly toured and had his own television show in Canada. In 1976 he flew to South Korea to make a one-off television programme for a Christian humanitarian organisation, World Vision, which had been set up during the conflict there in the 1950s to look after orphans.

However, he lost several points on the credibility-meter that same year when he toured South Africa, then at the most oppressive height of its apartheid system. Rolf's stance was doubly surprising given his publicly aired defence of Aboriginal culture in his homeland. The Nolan Sisters were the support act, and this encounter with the lasses from Blackpool resulted in them adding backing vocals to some of his tunes, including a version of 'Bargin' Down The Thames', a song he'd first aired on his TV show.

Rolf's always worked for good causes, something he's not always blown his own trumpet about. An acquaintance of Rolf's, who lived near the Harrises in the Sydenham area of South London in the 1970s, recalled a telling example of the singer's altruism. 'His kid went to school with my kids; we were on nodding and "how are you?" terms. A nice guy. He did things for the kids at the Eliot Bank School for no cost. Gained a reputation in the area for doing all things charitable without being stagey, such as fronting a local campaign (no national publicity) to get monies to send a small girl to America for an operation.

'Once, in the 1970s, I took a van load of fruit to sell at a fete at an autistic and Down Syndrome school. It cost me nothing; all monies for the school – in the Redhill area somewhere. Suddenly Rolf pulled into the school drive, estate car loaded with paint. Both surprised, we exchanged pleasantries. He was the celebrity, I sold fruit. He did this, starting at 11 am:

> Opened the swimming pool
> Fell into the swimming pool
> Painted a 20' x 30' mural on the wall
> Spoke and joked with every parent and kid
> Signed photos 50p each (for the school)
> Played instruments in the music room

'I fed him one or two drinks. At 5pm, he said "Can't give you a lift home, I'm on in cabaret at 8.00" (Caesar's Palace, Luton, I think). That man never charged a penny for his time and efforts.'

Charity work has had its knockers in the post-Smashy And Nicey era (Harry Enfield and Paul Whitehouse's satire of self-righteous radio personalities who pride themselves in their work for 'charidee, mate'), but Rolf's own efforts are genuine enough and later, in 1983, he was elected president of the Physically Handicapped and Able Bodied (PHAB) charity. He's also been a long-time supporter of the Royal National Institute for the Blind, and his most recent work for good causes has included the Vitas Gerulaitis Memorial Fund set up by fellow countryman and tennis star Pat Cash.

In 1977 he was rewarded for all his hard work both on and off-stage by being awarded with a second British honour – an OBE – and recalled the day of his investiture at Buckingham Palace with some pride in *Q*. 'When the Queen pinned on my OBE, she discussed my career with me with such knowledge about what I was doing, it was *unbelievable!* She knew the whole history of my career. It was bloody amazing!'

Rolf was still the tops with the kids. In the mid 1970s, a generation of teeny fans would wake up on Christmas morning to discover a copy of the latest Rolf Harris Annual tucked in their stockings amid the Donny Osmond socks or David Cassidy scarf! This contained the usual array of annual-type fun – jokes, games, puzzles, cartoon strips featuring Rolf and His Magic Brushes and Jake the Peg plus 'Snips From Rolf's Sketchbook' and activity features for children devised by Rolf himself. Best of all was the reproduction of some of his oil paintings such as his impression of the 'Two Little Boys'.

They could catch their hirsute hero on TV again when Rolf fronted *Rolf On Saturday – OK?* between 1977 and 1979, while its eponymous spin-off album containing classic children's songs such as 'Windmill In Amsterdam', 'The Laughing Policeman' and 'Boiled Beef And Carrots', took up residence on the decks of thousands of homes around the country.

Despite the success of *Rolf On Saturday – OK?*, it was his next series for the BBC for which he'll always be remembered. *Rolf Harris's Cartoon Time*, which ran regularly from 1979 to 1987, was a winning combination of classic animation from such famed studios as Warner Bros and Disney interspersed with Rolf's own dexterity in the painting and drawing department. It drew huge viewing figures and a whole generation of children were enchanted by his wizard skills and enthusiastic presentation of a subject close to his heart.

There may have been no 'Two Little Boys' to see out the 1970s, but in middle age Rolf was still clearly in demand. And there was always one more little surprise waiting for him around the corner. In 1979 he went back 'down under' to make his first feature film, *The Little Convict*. Directed by Yoram Gross – regarded as one of Australia's leading animators – this pleasant 80-minute long movie for kids was the tale of a little boy, Toby, who was shipped from London for a small misdemeanour – stealing food to survive the appalling poverty his family faced – to Botany Bay during the 19th Century as 'a guest of His Majesty's Government'. The film followed his adventures as he looked to find his freedom.

Set in New South Wales, the film was a mixture of live action and animation, and featured Rolf not only as narrator (the only 'human' role) but as the character Grandad, for which he had to undergo a complicated 'ageing process' in the make-up room every time he went before the camera! Talking about the film, he said, 'I love the story. For a start it's honest, it tells a little bit of the history of the country in a real way...it's entertaining without being a fairytale. I felt very real and believable in the role of the old bloke. What can I say? I love it!'

CHAPTER 4: SAVE THE ROLF

In 1980 Rolf, family and pets fittingly moved from their South London house to the ultra-posh surrounds of Bray-On-Thames, the celebrity neighbourhood in Berkshire frequented by figures of respectability like the Wogans and Parkinsons. His road to that select location had taken him a long way from the rabble-rousing pop world he'd inhabited back in the 1960s. It might have been a slog to get there, but Rolf had now reached the plateau of his career. He may not have wanted to hobnob with the stars of his own generation and their ilk, but nonetheless he still inhabited the same safe and cosy world and enjoyed a similar luxurious lifestyle as they did. And though he was an undoubted success, his position in the establishment was derided by some.

His credibility had already been put to the test a few years earlier by those anarchic funnymen the Goodies. Seen by some as the forerunners of 1980s alternative comedy, the trio of Tim Brooke-Taylor, Bill Oddie and Graeme Garden seem, from the vantage point of the late 1990s, rather less threatening. Oddie now spends his time as a keen ornithologist and environmentalist, while Taylor has tried his hand at sit-coms. Yet at the peak of their powers, the Goodies enjoyed nine massively popular seasons on both BBC and ITV, mercilessly pillorying establishment figures from the Royal Family to Radio One DJ John Peel who, in one programme, they claimed 'bored for Britain'. Justifiably or otherwise, Rolf also came into the line of fire, with a whole episode in the fifth series devoted to him. Titled *The Existence Of Rolf Harris*, it's said that Prince Charles allegedly offered to play himself!

Years later, Rolf admitted in Q that he'd become a subject of scorn and derision: 'I wasn't doing anything new in the 1970s. I stayed doing the same weirdie things and there wasn't much new creativity happening there. I was a sort of joke to a lot of people and some of those comments hurt. But what really hurt was Australian people saying, Oh, he's nothing more or less than a professional Australian. That's regarded as being a really heavy knock in Australia. When I had that enormous hit with "Kangaroo", that was the first genuine Australian accent-type song that had ever happened. What's wrong with that? Seemed a bloody good thing to me.'

Back in rock'n'roll circles, punk rock had briefly railed at the walls of the establishment. As with all youth cults, it had been squeezed into the mainstream and, in the cold light of the conservative 1980s, had become known as New Wave. Now one group who still revelled in the hedonism and irreverence of the original 1977 punk spirit was a band from the Croydon area who rejoiced under the suitably apt name of Splodgenessabounds! Unlikely saviours, they might have been, but they were about to give Rolf a boost in the credibility ratings.

The Splodges, known for outrageous onstage behaviour such as dropping their trousers and a distinctly lavatorial sense of humour in their repertoire, are best remembered for their wackily titled 'hit' 'Two Pints Of Lager And A Packet Of Crisps' which reached Number 7 in 1980. The band, totally rooted in 'pub culture' loved to joke and poke fun: among some of their funniest material were songs like 'I've Got Lots Of Famous People Living Under The Floorboards', 'Simon Templar' and 'Porky Scratchings'.

As it transpired, one of their biggest heroes was none other than Rolf Harris and to show their affection for their Antipodean idol, they recorded a fast and furious version of Rolf's greatest hit, 'Two Little Boys'. This was a real *tour de force* combining the original's lyrics with a great three-chord rock song, complete with a wobbleboard, a great sax solo refraining the beloved Aussie anthem 'Waltzing Matilda', what sounded suspiciously like a stylophone replacing the sombre trumpet voluntary at the end and something like a Jew's harp standing in for a didgeridoo.

The sentimental lyrics of the original became a classic punk rant and the Splodge's version's finest moment was the part where the wounded Joe, lying on the battlefield, cries out for help – which they turned into a wonderful football hooligan-style 'oi!' The single, released on the Deram label complete with the great catalogue number of ROLF 1, reached Number 26 in the UK listings on 6 September 1980. It even prompted EMI to reissue the original via its HMV off-shoot, but this time it didn't reach the charts.

But Splodgenessabounds' idolatry of the bearded one didn't end there – they even went as far as to write their own tribute song to him, simply titled 'Rolf'. A perennial favourite in their live set, it finally reached vinyl on their eponymous 1981 album, also on Deram. Tongue-in-cheek perhaps, 'Rolf' was certainly another power-chorded punk song in the vein of the Sex Pistols and Adverts, but far from ridiculing its subject the lyrics were unashamedly in praise of the bespectacled entertainer.

The group was always happy to push Rolf's name in interviews with the weekly pop press, and there was a small groundswell of pro-Rolf mania from like-minded bands with an amazing end result – a special show, Save The Rolf, staged at the Tramshed in Woolwich. Another figure from the punk era who liked Rolf was John Otway, an Aylesbury musician who'd been discovered by the Who's Pete Townshend and (with sidekick Wild Willy Barrett) had made the charts with 'Cor Baby, That's Really Free'.

Like Splodgenessabounds, Otway was fond of reworking classic old hits like Tom Jones's 'The Green Green Grass Of Home' and in the late 1980s, began to feature his own energetic, punkified take of 'Two Little Boys' in his live act. He finally released the song in 1992 as a single but it failed to chart. However his connection with Rolf didn't quite end there as his erstwhile partner-in-crime, guitarist and fiddler Wild Willy, later joined Harris's backing band!

In 1981, Rolf found himself hosting a TV programme at Ancaster High School in Lincoln. As was his wont, his quick-fire sketches were inspired by his surroundings, and when the programme was well and truly 'wrapped' he gave two of them, a Lincolnshire poacher complete with a haul of rabbits and a portrait of a local countryman in a flat cap, to the school. Rolf thought of these as 'rehearsal exercises', but they were fairly large ones at eight feet by seven feet – and so proud was the school of them that they displayed them prominently in the hall.

Unfortunately, time took its inevitable toll on these magnificent 'murals' and, after 16 years of exposure to light and central heating – not to mention inquisitive pupils! – they were beginning to show signs of fading. 'We are seeking expert advice as to how to preserve them,' explained school secretary Maureen Bailey, and art restorer Bart Luckhurst was engaged to ensure the 'didgeridoodles' would be round to enthral and captivate future generations of children. 'I shouldn't think Rolf had intended his pictures to have as long a life as this,' he mused while inspecting the historic artworks. Rolf, for his part, professed himself 'very flattered' at the trouble taken.

As the 1980s wore on, Rolf's lot was a mixed one. He was busy with his on-going *Cartoon Time* but his light entertainment programme, *Rolf's Here – OK?* ran for only six episodes in 1981 before the BBC cancelled any further series. By the same token, as an internationally renowned celebrity, he was constantly on call to present all manner of events around the globe. In 1982 he was busy representing his home country at the Knoxville Expo in the US and just a few months later, he recorded a TV special to herald the start of the Commonwealth Games in Brisbane. (He'd also take part in the special gala show in Edinburgh in front of the Queen and Prince Philip in aid of the 1986 Games.)

In 1983, he recorded a similar one-off show to mark the the triumphant return of the Australia II team who'd just won the Americas Cup, and he represented Australia in an American TV spectacular prefacing the 1984 Olympic Games in Los Angeles. When Australia celebrated its bicentennial in 1988, the ubiquitous Rolf was inevitably among those leading the nation's celebrations – and how! Seemingly able to be in three places at once, he presented the first event from New South Wales, an international scout jamboree, following this up by a prestigious appearance before Prince Charles and the late Princess Diana at a Bicentennial Royal Command Performance in Sydney. He also compered a concert for a gathering of tall ships in Hobart, Tasmania before they set off for Sydney.

Rolf had sporadically released singles since his 1960s heyday, but titles like 'Hey Jimmy Johnson' b/w 'Ginger Tom' put out by RHE in November 1981 had failed to capture the record-buying public's imagination. However, in 1985 he momentarily re-appeared in the British singles charts, albeit as part of a major group effort.

This was the era of the charity record, as spearheaded by ex-punk Bob Geldof and his work for Ethiopian famine victims under the Band Aid/Live Aid banner. In the spring of 1985, there'd been a major disaster at Bradford City Football Club when a stand had caught fire and claimed the lives of over 50 people. In its aftermath a number of pop musicians and top flight entertainers came together collectively as The Crowd to record a benefit record for the relatives of those who'd died and to assist the club to recover from the tragedy.

Led by Gerry Marsden, they recorded Rodgers & Hammerstein's 'You'll Never Walk Alone' – a song which Gerry and his band, the Pacemakers had taken to Number 1 in October 1963. Such was the British public's concern that people went out in droves and sent the single, co-produced by 10CC's Graham Gouldman, to Number 1 for two weeks in June 1985. Rolf was one of those lending his vocal support along with the likes of the Nolans, the late Phil Lynott, Bernie Winters, Bruce Forsyth and Rose Marie, while Ringo Starr's son Zak was on the drums. Eighteen months later, Tembo Records put out a new Rolf single, 'Tommy (From '88 Pines)' but again there was no surge of interest from the public and the single flopped.

In Australia, meanwhile, his TV series continued to do well while back in the UK the 1980s saw him make his debut in pantomime – something that was to become a regular Yuletide fixture for Rolf. His first appearance in panto was as Buttons in *Cinderella* at the Lewisham Theatre in his old stamping ground of south-east London over Christmas 1982. He obviously developed a real appetite for this kind of work because he reprised the role in Bournemouth in 1985 and again in Richmond in 1986.

He gently satirised Paul Hogan's legendary Crocodile Dundee character with his own version of the all-Australian action hero – 'Rough Rolf' – in *Mother Goose* in Hull in 1988. The tradition continued with a role in *Aladdin* in Eastbourne in 1990, but in the late 1980s Rolf sometimes had to take the rough with the smooth and during a winter tour of the provinces, an appearance at Blackpool's Grand Theatre attracted only a handful of people. It must have been one of the few low points of his career.

On the other hand, the date of 26 January 1989 must have ranked as one of the most triumphant in his career so far. On 'Australia Day', he was accorded the supreme honour – Member of the Order of Australia – which recognised his 'unique talents and services to so many individuals and causes' and 'for services to the community as an entertainer.' Of the award, Rolf said, 'We Australians tend to treat this sort of thing as happening to somebody else, but deep down inside, it's a terrific feeling.' It was the start of a good year for Rolf.

A follow-up to his 1969 series, *Rolf's Walkabout – 20 Years Down The Track*, was screened and in April he began a new TV run. Cartoon Time had ended in 1987 with BBC Records releasing a soundtrack memento of the series, *Cartoon Time Favourites*. This was a cornucopia of singalong favourites from the golden age of animation – evergreens like 'Zip-a-dee-doo-dah', 'Whistle While You Work' and

One of Rolf's early promotional shots, circa 1963

Rolf with similarly striking shirt and tie, 1964

Fooling around, 1965

The family man

Jake the Peg

'Can you tell what it is yet?'

The wobbleboard - every self-respecting Rock God should have one

Didgereely do that?

Cartoon capers with Rolf

Rolf showing off his animal magnetism

Rolf Harris...the most talented man in the world?

'Bare Necessities' – a treat for both children discovering them for the first time around and for mums and dads who'd heard the originals at the cinema.

The end of the series made him decide it was time to try something fresh, and *Rolf's Cartoon Club* – complete with a revamped format – was launched on the independent network in April 1989. 'I've always enjoyed working with the BBC,' he commented, 'but it's really time for a change. With HTV, we plan a whole range of new programmes giving me the chance to demonstrate abilities other than those I'm already known for.'

As ever, Rolf was much in demand in Australia that year and to offset the tedium of flying back and forth across that continent he began to write his first novel – in freehand – during the flights! Following in the footsteps of other recent Rolf publications such as *A Catalogue Of Comic Verse* and *Your Cartoon Time*, a spin-off from his much-loved TV series,*Win Or Die: The Making Of A King* was bound to be a success.

Hodder & Stoughton published it in time for the festive season. Aimed very much with children in mind, the story followed the adventures of young King Alonzo who escapes the confines of his court to see what it's like in the 'real' world. The young royal is pronounced dead and his throne taken by the evil Count Tzlenko – Alonzo has to somehow struggle back, and finds help in the unlikely company of some gypsies. It was an endearing tale that Rolf had spent considerable time researching – especially the parts about pottery-making, bee-keeping, fencing and swordplay – and he based some of the main characters on friends and acquaintances. His Uncle Olaf was the raw material for Silvander the Potter and drummer Keith Harrison the basis for Old Roger, while air hostess Sonya Bell was, in Rolf's own words, 'just perfect for Queen Alice'.

The Ansett airline company she worked for and which had ferried Rolf so safely to so many live dates during that period received their own special acknowledgement. They had apparently let Rolf use the NEC fax machine in their Golden Wing lounges and he had been able to transmit 30 pages or more at a time of the novel directly to his London publisher free of charge! The illustrations, mainly done in pen and ink and executed by the man himself, were superbly evocative with a very Mervyn Peake Gormenghastian feel about them: they'd been drawn at the house of Clifton Pugh in Victoria.

The novel had a very interesting genesis. Back in 1969 Rolf and family had spent time with naturalists Harry Butler and Vin and Carol Serventy in the Northern Territory of Australia where they made the series *Rolf's Walkabout* for ABC (it was later picked up and repeated by the BBC). There were quite a few children in the party, including Rolf's daughter Bindi, and each evening at bedtime, Harris would tell them a bedtime story, making up a new episode each night.

He had no plans to develop them into a proper book until one day in 1975 he visited Joanne Whitney who ran a pottery kiln in Lyndhurst near Bournemouth. It was there at Angel Farm that he also met Joanne's dad Roland, now retired, who was a skilled and enthusiastic beekeeper and they'd hit off straightaway. Bees and pottery had been 'key ingredients' of those original goodnight stories and Rolf remembered thinking, as he put it in *Win Or Die*, 'if I ever write that yarn I'll get a tape recorder and sit down with this marvellous man and make sure I get the facts right.' Sadly, by the time Rolf did finally sit down to put pen to paper, Roland had died…but as a mark of respect both to him and the four children 'who were such good listeners', he dedicated the book to the family.

CHAPTER 5: STAIRWAY TO HEAVEN

For most people, entering their 60th year of life would normally mean putting on the brakes. But not so with Rolf Harris. Life in 1990 was as hectic as ever and it was business as usual. The second series of *Cartoon Club* was under way and, as an unexpected but welcome spin-off, Rolf found himself in Hollywood visiting some of the fabled animation studios there to film a Christmas special. He was also commissioned by Australian television to go to India to film *Rolf's Indian Walkabout*, later broadcast around the globe – the thought of all those mouthwatering curries no doubt made him jump at the chance! And he rounded off the year with another pantomime role, this time in *Aladdin* in Eastbourne.

Rolf was still spending up to three or four months of every year in Australia and 1991 was no exception as he went on a nationwide tour there, including many cabaret spots. Back in England, a fourth series of *Cartoon Club* was ready to roll – the series had been nominated the previous year by the Royal Television Society's Best Factual Programme award. To coincide with its broadcast, his old record label EMI lined up some back-catalogue material for public consumption.

The compact disc had now taken over from vinyl

as the music industry's preferred format and, as each disc could hold up to 80 minutes of material, many of the major companies were raiding their vaults to re-release classic old stuff. Through the Ideal imprint, they'd already released the eponymous 'Rolf Harris' the previous February. This was a trip through Rolf's early past as a recording artist and naturally contained all his hits as well as more obscure items such as 'Maximillian Mouse' and his version of 'English Country Garden'. The CD boasted five extra tracks by comparison with the vinyl original, including 'Sydney Town' and 'Man With The Microphone'.

On 21 October 1991, EMI released a 'new' Rolf single – the great 'Sun Arise'. The fourth run of *Cartoon Club* would follow a group of children creating a cartoon to illustrate various parts of the classic song during which Rolf showed both them and viewers the basic elements of animation and the use of computer graphics. The 7-inch and cassette formats both contained additional cuts, 'Two Little Boys' and 'Six White Boomers' while the CD boasted the wonderful 'I've Lost My Mummy'. 'Six White Boomers' was an interesting choice – it had been written back at the start of the 1960s when Rolf was running his first kids' shown for Australian TV.

As anyone with even a scant knowledge of geography knows, there's not much snow down under during Yuletide, and Rolf was forced to come up with something equivalent to 'Rudolph The Red-Nosed Reindeer'. Rolf recalled the song's genesis when introducing *Didgereely-Doo All That?*

'In Perth, Western Australia in 1960, one of the staff of the television station I was working for was an American named John D Brown. He thought it was crazy to be singing Christmas songs about snow and ice with everyday temperatures around the 100 degrees Fahrenheit. Consequently we got together one Sunday morning with a huge sheet of paper spread out on his lounge floor, and over the next four hours, with numerous re-writes and rubbings out, we created this old, old, old "Australian Christmas Legend".' Neither album nor single charted but they were the first signs that a big revival of interest in the man with the marker pen was imminent.

Life trucked evenly along as ever – more panto, this time in Aberdeen, preparations for a fifth series of his cartoon programme and more work overseas. However, in 1992 he was given a huge boost when a straw poll taken among 1,000 Londoners asked them to name a painter. Rembrandt and Turner didn't even get a look in, Constable only took 23 per cent of the vote while the most frequently cited, with a staggering 38 per cent, was none other than Rolf Harris!

Talking of his success in *Q*, Rolf observed, 'It's

amazing, isn't it? It's the power of television. I mean, did Rembrandt do any paintings on television? He probably didn't. But, you see, art galleries have got a little bit of an elitist feel about them, whereas people can look at at me painting from scratch, from a blank canvas and they go, Oh wow! It helps them to understand the finished process and it encourages them.'

Added to this was the unexpected honour of having a Students Union Building named in his honour. Back in the 1980s, as a token of respect and solidarity, there'd been a wave of campuses around the UK which had taken the unprecedented step of naming their student bars or halls after jailed South African freedom fighter Nelson Mandela. It was a small mark of liberal protest in a hard-line right-wing era. But by the early 1990s, there was a whole new generation of students out there, who no longer felt the flicker of protest their mums and dads or older brothers and sisters had – after all, most students were now in the unenviable position of having to pay their grants or loans back upon graduation.

In 1992, the students at the University of Warwick voted overwhelmingly to change their Students Union Bar's name to the Rolf Harris Room. As he recalled in *Q*, 'they held a meeting and 95 per cent of the students union voted for the Rolf Harris Room. That was magic! I went up there and presented a painting of me as a kangaroo and I entertained them with every song I'd ever thought of singing with no musical accompaniment and all these great big strapping youngsters were joining in because 'Two Little Boys' was the first record they remembered. And then I signed autographs for about two and half hours. The queue was just going on forever. I was absolutely shattered, but it's a lovely feeling.'

It was however a case of swings and roundabouts, however, as HTV decided to end *Cartoon Club* after the fifth series. 'They say you shouldn't appear with children or animals,' he'd later admit to *Radio Times*, 'but that only applies if you want to be the big star. I've always liked to stand aside and let them shine. I hate to see them as unpaid moving background, which happens too much. I was upset the programme ended. I was 62 and assumed I might as well pack it in.'

There were those who believed that, in view of his popularity as a painter, he should have stuck solely to that course since his art-school days – and, talking to *Radio Times*, he seemed to agree. 'I wish I was just an artist,' he reflected. 'Yes, I sure do. I wonder where I would have gone if I had developed my painting. I watched Cliff Richard the other night in concert and and thought there was a man who pursued one goal to perfection. I'd never have had the strength of purpose to suffer so much, though.'

However, something happened during 1992 that would lead to the relaunch of Rolf's career on a trajectory not even the canniest of managers could have predicted. A 'new wave comedy' show called *The Money Or The Gun* had been enjoying huge ratings on Australian television, with a zany mixture of live bands and studio audience participation. One of its most successful features was the part of the show which invited a wide range of guests to perform a version of Led Zeppelin's pompous rock anthem 'Stairway To Heaven'.

The song – a lengthy epic that addressed the subject of a spiritual quest – had originally been recorded for the band's 1971 masterpiece 'Led Zeppelin IV' and was widely regarded by hard rock and heavy metal fans as one of the finest songs ever written. The tune had even been released as a disco-fied single in the 1980s. Among the 'victims' who'd performed it on *The Money Or The Gun* were tribute bands the Australian Doors and the Rock Lobsters, the Sydney Philharmonia, Vegemite Reggae and Kate Ceberano. The many versions which included reggae, operatic, heavy metal and lounge jazz were later collected together on an album released by Vertigo in 1992 logically entitled 'Stairways To Heaven'.

Rolf recalled his invitation to appear on the show

in the liner notes to *Didgereely-Doo All That?* 'I was touring Australia doing my normal sort of concert with all the songs I do, the stories, the jokes and the big paintings. While I was in Sydney, Stuart White who handles publicity there for me, was also doing PR for Andrew Denton, a very successful TV presenter. His comedy show *The Money Or The Gun* was nearing the end of a very long, very successful run and Stuart thought it would be good promotion for my tour if I did the musical spot on the show. I'd seen a bit of one of the shows and really liked Andrew's zany approach, so I agreed.

'Then they told me they wanted me to sing "Stairway To Heaven", and I'd never heard of it. They just couldn't believe me.

"But it's a Led Zeppelin classic!" they stammered.

"Ah well nothing to do with me," I said. "Couldn't I sing one of my own songs?"

"No, you don't understand," they replied. "It's the policy of the show. The only song we ever sing is 'Stairway.' So far we've had 19 different versions of it, from an Elvis Presley impersonation to an operatic interpretation with a huge symphony orchestra. We've had heavy-metal versions, someone even did it as a poem, and we'd like to do the definitive Rolf Harris version with everything that says 'Rolf Harris' to the public. We'll send you a copy of the original recording to listen to."

'I said I didn't want to hear what anyone else had

done with the song. I really would prefer to work out what I was going to do from just seeing the sheet music.'

Rolf unconsciously then proceeded to do the ultimate deconstruction of the number. Working with his musical director, Clive Lendich, and backing musicians, he totally re-arranged the song. Gone were the macho drum figures that John Bonham produced to give the original its backbone, and gone too was Jimmy Page's heavy-metal guitar. In their place was a hesitant accordion, and the instantly recognisable Harris hallmarks – the wobbleboard and didgeridoo.

The way he performed the lyrics was astounding: some verses were completely expunged, while Rolf added his own little asides, even pretending to misinterpret one line, splitting the word misgiven into 'Miss Given' and asking her to take a curtain call. It was a magnificent achievement – and, by performing it as a kind of 'Tie Me Kangaroo Down Sport' for the 1990s, he both celebrated the original and at the same time punctured its pompous self-regard like a scalpel. He'd later say of the rendition, 'I'm busy mocking myself all the way through.'

His permission to include the song on the compilation was duly given and he forgot all about it. Unbeknown to him his version became the jewel in the album's crown, and an immediate hit on radio stations all over Australia with the public demanding its release as a single. A copy somehow found its way over to England and eventually reached BBC DJ Simon Bates, who in late 1992 was holding down the mid-morning spot on Radio One. He took an immediate shine to it and started playing it every day for nearly three weeks – an honour not even accorded 'Two Little Boys'. His audience loved it and the pressure grew to issue it in the UK. The first Rolf knew about the furore was in Bath, where he was appearing in pantomime.

The Vertigo label caved into pressure and released the single in February 1993 with Rolf going all out to promote it on TV and in concert. Not normally a gambling man, he was so delighted by its success that he even placed a bet of £100 that the song would return him to Number 1. Said William Hill, the bookies, 'we offered Rolf special odds of 10-1 because it's his record and he's giving his winnings to charity', while Ladbroke's commented, 'We're praying that Rolf's terrible re-make won't get to Number 1. We could lose more than £35,000.' The 'Stairway' single faced stiff competition from the likes of Take That and Whitney Houston and the then-current chart-topper by 2 Unlimited. It shot straight into the Number 9 position in the first week of its release peaking just two places higher.

Nonetheless, Rolf was thrilled to be back in the public eye as a hit recording artist who had caught the imagination of a whole new generation of record-buyers. In *The Sun*, he enthused, 'I can't believe I'm a pop star again. I feel like I'm still 22, the same age I was when I came to Britain…it's incredible the way it's all taken off again. I have never run so fast as I have this week. I thought all this sort of thing was behind me. But I don't remember being half as busy last time. It has all happened so suddenly.

"My family keep telling me to ease up because of my age. They say I should take things easier and have one day each week which I can spend quietly with them. I promised to take it easier and take some time off to do some painting. But I'm a workaholic. I can't say no to anybody – like people who want to interview me. I've still got half my autobiography to write, another book to illustrate, which is behind deadline, and I'm off to Australia next week to promote my single.'

Scarcely drawing breath, Rolf was soon enjoying a similar success with the record in his home country. It had obviously struck a nerve with the younger generation. Far from being an aberration, those students at Warwick University had merely been the first to welcome Rolf back in from the cold. He was soon in demand as an unlikely performer on the college circuit, a position that was cemented by an appearance at the 1993 Glastonbury Festival in Somerset over the summer solstice in June.

Though more a cultural celebration than just a mega rock bash, Glastonbury usually played host to the popular young rock bands of the day – by the 1990s, tickets for the weekend costing over £60 per person usually sold out weeks in advance such was interest in it. 1993 boasted a line up which included Suede, the Orb and chief Lemonhead Evan Dando. One of the surprise success stories of the 1992 festival had been an appearance by another 1960s throwback, Tom Jones. However, when Rolf appeared, his performance totally eclipsed that of the aging Welshman.

As he recalled in his '*Best Of*' sleevenotes, 'I was extremely nervous when I arrived and saw the size of the crowd, as you can imagine, but the hardened backstage crew really relaxed me when they said, "you're the only one we want to hear mate! Are you gonna be doing 'Jake The Peg' and 'Two Little Boys'?" When I came onstage, the reaction was electric, and that huge audience sang every word of every song with me at "football-crowd" level. The volume of sound was such that I sang right through "Sun Arise" in a different key to the band, and was never aware of it. The good feelings of love and affection that poured out to me from all those thousands of people, made that day one of the highlights of my life!'

Indeed, Rolf was the undoubted star of the whole event. Resplendent in a biker jacket with his dependable wobbleboard and didgeridoo at the ready, he wowed the 80,000-strong audience with a selection of favourites, getting a special roar when he did his 'Jake' routine complete with third leg, while the sight of the crowd, 18 to 60 year olds all singing along to 'Two Little Boys' – once ridiculed by any self-respecting rock fan – must have brought tears to his eyes. 'They knew every word,' he recalled. 'It was bloody marvellous.'

And there was an apposite footnote to the whole 'Stairway' saga. Led Zeppelin had split up in 1980 but in 1994, its two main protagonists, singer Robert Plant and guitarist Jimmy Page who'd originally written the song, re-united for a fine 'unplugged' album 'No Quarter – Unledded' which combined more traditional Led Zep rockers with various world music styles. And they took a band out on the road complete with Moroccan musicians, which turned in an excellent set on the Glastonbury Pyramid Stage, a year after Rolf's stupendous debut there.

There seemed to be no doubt that the aging Antipodean's record had partly at least been at the root of this reunion. Rolf told *Goldmine* that he'd yet to meet them but he'd seen the pair on television, 'I was in Bundaberg and they were in Sydney, I would have liked to have met them! They said we all grew up on Rolf on TV when we were kids, there was a nice atmosphere.' Page and Plant finished that Sydney TV appearance by returning the compliment and dusting off their own very special version of Rolf's 'Sun Arise' complete with didgeridoo!

As a result of his rapturous reception at Glastonbury, he was booked to appear at the Edinburgh Festival, where his contract actually stipulated that he had to perform an all-song set which included all his big hits. It was clearly a thrill. Talking about his appearance in *The Guardian's* Festival Diary, he wrote: 'Last night I got back here at about two in the morning, and I was on such a high that I couldn't sleep. There was so much excitement and creative buzz. Fancy a show starting at 12 midnight! You think, "What? Is anybody going to be there?" I was in a bit of a panic last night thinking "Nobody's going to turn up", but it was three-quarters full and jumping with excitement. The audience were absolutely bloody marvellous.'

So, at 63, Rolf was 'hipper' than at any previous stage of his life and he was taking it all in his stride. Pantomime appearances were still part and parcel of this seasoned entertainer's calendar – in 1993, it was the role of Simple Simon in *Jack And The Beanstalk* in Plymouth, but he was now also the toast of the university circuit. He enthused in *Radio Times*, 'I was told by a friend that his son and mates went to see me at Aberdeen University as a gag but found it an hour-and-a-half of bloody good entertainment. They arrived to mock and remained to enjoy. Now it's like Beatlemania all over again, a tremendous ego boost for me. When I visit universities, they shout, "We love you, Rolfie, Rolfie, we love you" – I join in. They seem to know every word to every song I've ever done.' 'Stairway' had in the great man's own words, 'given that age group permission to admit they really like me, which they hadn't dared say until then.'

EMI obviously saw they had a new target audience and re-released a 23-song greatest hits package on 17 May 1994 entitled *Didgereely-Doo All That?* that chronologically featured all his hits to date including 'Stairway'. It came with some excellent sleevenotes by Rolf himself. Much of the year was taken up by club gigs and personal appearances such as opening the Southport Flower Show – the reception to which, he told *Night And Day*, 'was like being king of the world for an hour.' And his opening a major horticultural event was no mismatch either. For years he and wife and Alwen have managed to successfully cultivate various specimens of Australian flora in their garden at Bray – no small feat given the hostile British climate!

He also had a consistently full sheet of live club dates, a review of his gig at the Plymouth Warehouse in autumn 1994 in *Making Music* magazine confirming that he was, as ever, on top form. 'Rolf walked on stage in a long coat, sporting an extra leg, all set to break into "Jake The Peg",' the reviewer remarked, 'only to be drowned out by cheering. The enthusiasm was infectious and the atmosphere sent a warm glow through everybody. Even the Russian and English version of "Tie Me Kangaroo Down Sport" couldn't dilute the concentrated euphoria that had built up. The other classics sounded equally brilliant, only two cartoons were drawn, and there was plenty of amusing between-song patter.'

However, for one dark period that year, it looked as if it might all be over for the man who was enjoying a real second coming. It was rumoured that all the extra pressures of renewed success in his mid-60s had allegedly caused a nervous breakdown. 'It wasn't that so much as a viral infection which caused terrible vertigo,' he revealed later to *Radio Times*. 'I couldn't stay upright. I thought my brain was going. They put me in hospital and filled me full of Cortisone, which kept me awake for 24 hours a day, raring to go. When they finally took me off the pills I had terrible depression.

'I'm always the life and soul of the party and love everyone but suddenly, dear oh dear, I was down in the dumps, suicidal for a while. I understand why people jump off bridges. I felt as low as ever and didn't see how I'd recover. My wife couldn't bear to be near me and I was snappy with everyone. Nothing was right. Doctors told me to take pills to counteract it, but I didn't want any more of the bloody things so I had to wait until it all cleared up on its own, which took about six weeks.'

Which was fortunate, because Rolf was now about to be catapulted back into the public eye on a massive scale.

CHAPTER 6: ANIMAL HOSPITAL

In August 1994, the BBC launched a one-off special television series. Broadcast each evening live from the RSPCA's Sir Harold Harmsworth Memorial Hospital in Holloway, North London, *Animal Hospital Live*. It started on Bank Holiday Monday 29 August and, for the next five nights, the TV cameras brought the trials and tribulations – as they happened – to the pets, their owners, and the vets who treated them, directly into the homes of viewers all over the country. And presenting the programme with his usual cheery and sympathetic style was none other than Rolf Harris!

As an animal lover, he'd jumped at the opportunity to work on the series. At the end of the previous year, he and Alwen had collaborated on a book entitled *Personality Cats*. This was something of a labour of love and was inspired by the Harrises' fascination with the breed of cat known as the Devon Rex – a skinny-looking moggie with enormous ears, hardly any body hair and tiny face, making it resemble nothing more than extra terrestrial!

Talking to *Midland News Association*, Rolf waxed, 'they're completely unlike any other cat we've ever seen. They behave like dogs in a way, in that they always want to be with you. They follow you around all the time, they love nothing better than to sit on your shoulder. Most cats are independent, but if Alwen goes out into the garden the Devon Rexes all troop out with her. Because of the thin fur you haven't got the insulation effect when you pick them up, you actually feel the body heat. They always feel very hot, almost as if they have a fever.' *Personality Cats*, he commented, 'was all about the ones we've had in our married life, with drawings I've done of them and photographs I've taken. You just wouldn't believe how many boxes of slides of our cats I've got!'

Though he readily admits that animals have never been an obsession with him, he's always had an involvement with them – the Harris household boasts two Devon Rexes, Beetle and Toffee, a Standard poodle called Summers and most recently a Bengal cat. And he knows both the happy and sad experiences people can have keeping them. 'When I was about nine,' he told one interviewer, 'I had a dog run over and killed right in front of me. Then we had a dog die after eating poison bait. Another dog we had when I was about 15 also got poisoned but I saved him by mixing some warm salt water and forcing it down his throat to make him sick. I managed to bring him round eventually and he was okay, so it was a great thrill to be able to do that.'

Just prior to recording the first series of *Animal Hospital*, Rolf had to undergo the heartbreak of one of his beloved Devon Rexes dying. 'We had another named Toad', he told BBC reporter Mark Barden, 'who was Toffee's brother, but one morning when I was away working, my wife Alwen got up and found the poor little thing was dead. We were absolutely devastated. We had an autopsy done on him and we were told it was viral pneumonia. Toffee was absolutely lost for a while because they used to play together all the time.

'We felt awful, but you have to realise that birth, living and death are all part of a cycle. You should never just get a pet for the good times, but you should enjoy the life of that animal and be aware that their lifecycle is shorter than ours and that there's going to be sadness at the end of it. When a pet dies, I think the best thing to do is get another one straight away if you can manage it.'

With such a clear philosophy, Rolf looked like he'd been waiting for this role all his life. 'It's not our job on *Animal Hospital Live* to wallow in sentimentality,' he claimed. 'We want to give viewers an insight into everyday life here and show them what a fantastic job the RSPCA do at the Harmsworth.' And, as the series started, he appeared to be willing to handle whatever creature came his way. 'Rats are quite nice,' he admitted to Barden, 'they're incredibly intelligent and can be great pets. Alwen kept them when she was a girl. I *used* to be frightened of snakes until I was given some hard facts by a person who's very at ease with them and I handled a non-poisonous one.'

The only type of animal he wasn't inclined to deal with was the dreaded arachnid. 'I'm not too good with spiders. We used to have trapdoor spiders in our garden in Australia when I was a little kid and I was forever watching them sitting there then closing their trapdoors as I approached. They fascinated me, but I must say my reaction to spiders these days is to put a glass over them, slide a piece of cardboard underneath, take them outside and go... (mimics someone with a bad case of arachnophobia). It's just the speed they move towards you when you don't want them to...If someone comes in with a big spider and they can talk me into it, I'll have a go at holding it – though, as it's going out live, I think I'd be more terrified about accidentally pulling one of its legs off!'

Co-presented by Lynda Bryans and Steve Knight, the programme was an immediate hit with British viewers, obviously striking a deep chord with a nation of animal lovers. And that it was transmitted live added a great spontaneous edge – 'Live TV is great,' enthused Rolf, himself a consummate live performer. 'It has an electricity that pre-recorded stuff just doesn't have, just by virtue of the fact it's happening live now and you've got no other chance to get it right except this once. The old adrenalin really starts pumping. If something disastrous happens, you've just got to somehow get yourself out of it. You've got to own up, be as real as you can under the circumstances and deal with it.'

After the first series, there was a special Christmas programme and such was the universal thumbs-up that it returned in January 1995 for a further nine weeks. It drew an audience of 11 million, challenging ITV's *The Bill* for top placing in the Thursday night ratings. Such was its popularity that the second series was extended for an extra four weeks, finishing on Rolf's 65th birthday – and, during part of its run the indefatigable trouper was doing two performances a day in panto as Baron Hardup in *Cinderella* in Wimbledon as well as fronting the programme!

Talking of the show's appeal in *Radio Times*, its producer Lorraine Heggessey said of its main presenter, 'He's a tremendous asset. He identifies very much with the plight of the animals and their owners and that sincerity comes across to the audience. Rolf is the only presenter I can think of who could be in tears on camera while hugging a man he had never met before, comforting him when his dog had to be put down.'

But even Rolf would be the first to admit that the animals are the true stars and the vets the real heroes! Veterinarians like headman David Grant have to be as professional on air as Rolf himself is and carry out often difficult surgery – tough tasks with the cameras on them all the time. During the second series for example, David had to appear before the nation calmly dealing with the usual animal ailments while putting aside his personal concerns about his newly-born daughter.

'Laura was six weeks premature in the special care unit at Edgware General,' he told *Radio Times*, 'They had her on a respirator breathing 100 per cent oxygen, with morphine to stop her pulling out the tubes. I couldn't sleep sometimes and I'd go there at two in the morning to see how she was.' She eventually pulled through but it had been 'extremely difficult' for David to be up bright-eyed and bushy-tailed the next morning to face the cameras. In the same series, he was also faced with the task of having to put down an old dog, Barney whom he'd saved 15 years before from being an unwanted puppy.

'He was on the table just about to be put down and I remembered him and offered to take him home. He was old and going downhill. His kidneys had failed, and the rest of it. It's natural to cry when your pet is put to sleep. He was a nice dog; I couldn't help it. There's no doubt that it's different when it's your own dog. About two days later I drove home and parked in the drive and clicked the catch for the boot to let Barney out. And, of course, he wasn't there. That upset me a little but I was so busy, there were so many things going on, including *Animal Hospital*, that I didn't have the luxury of moping about it.'

The programme was voted by viewers as the Most Popular Factual Entertainment Show at the first National Television Awards in 1995. Talking about why it had made such a major impact, Rolf observed in *Radio Times*, 'It's real animals, real people, real problems and real vets. Plus me being as real as I can within the confines of the fact it's television. You can still be real in your emotional reaction and mirror what the person at home is thinking.'

He cited the case of Floss the dog who'd collapsed from heart failure, the vet telling its young owner that it was kinder to put her to sleep, 'the owner, a lad, burst into tears. I gave him a cuddle. And then they had a shot of the old dog taking a last look over its shoulder. It was heart-rending. I doubt there was a dry eye in the country.' Indeed on several occasions, viewers saw Rolf wipe away a tear – not exactly the normal public reaction of somebody who comes from a country renowned for its macho 'pom-bashing' maleness, where it just simply isn't done for men to be seen crying.

'The British find human relationships difficult because they are inward looking, shy and formal,' Rolf explained to *Radio Times*: 'The expression of emotion is not encouraged, so it's bottled up – the same as in Australia when I was young. Boys don't cry, and all that stupidity. Crying is a wonderful release of tension. Quite often an animal is a safety valve that allows us to express the wonderful love within us all. You can lavish it on a dog or cat, particularly if you are a single person living alone, rather than go into a human relationship with all the tensions of whether or not it's going to work out. It's a lot safer to love an animal because it won't break your heart.'

CHAPTER 7: SMOKE ON THE WATER

It was a wonder that in 1995 with the sudden take-off of *Animal Hospital Live* that Rolf had much time for anything else – there were always family matters to take care. In May, Rolf must have looked proudly on as daughter Bindi carried on the family tradition and had her first exhibition of paintings displayed at London's Candid Gallery. Her mum and dad had noticed her abilities from an early age, even allowing her to draw and scribble on the walls of their South London home to nurture her fledgling talents an artist. A portrait painted by her of mum Alwen takes centre stage in the Harris homestead in Bray. Talking of her work, she commented 'my pictures are very emotional and impressionistic...absolutely nothing like Dad's except that they're big,' while Rolf, conscious of his own rating in that recent opinion poll, modestly ventured, 'I don't think people think I'm better than Rembrandt...but Bindi might keep them on their toes.'

In June, he celebrated the release of a new compact disc album by Music Collection International. The music it contained was something of a departure, for him but in keeping with his recent rock'n'roll successes, *'Rolf Rules OK'* – the title a neat echo of one of his old TV series –

was a selection of interpretations of 1970s hard-rock classics! Rolf didn't necessarily like some of the latest trends in pop music: as he told *The Sun*, 'I don't like rap and get lost with most of today's songs. I like songs with a story in them and a lyric you can follow.'

But even if many of today's pop acts didn't measure up to Rolf's demanding standards, he admitted he did have a sneaking admiration for Madonna. 'Madonna is the greatest publicity machine in the world. I think she is outrageous intentionally. I saw her book (*Sex*) and thought the photographs were quite exquisite. I thought it was very nicely handled and there was very little that was crude or pornographic.' He didn't have the courage to take on 'Like A Virgin' but he did get to grips with some hard-riffing rock.

The album had been recorded at the Megaphon Studios in Sydney in the excitement of the 'Stairway' single's assault on the chart during February/March 1993, and had been masterminded by his brother. 'Bruce got hold of me when I was back in Sydney and said, "why not get as many old rock'n'roll favourites, top songs as we can and record them in your style",' he told *Goldmine*. 'Clive Lendich, my musical director, drew up a short list of songs. Some famous, like the Rolling Stones, but others I hadn't heard before. "Gosh, I can't sing those in a million years!" I said,

"They're nothing to do with me". "Yes you can", came the reply. "Do it your way, put your stamp on it – make it sound like you".'

Recalling the making of the album, Rolf told *Goldmine* that the studio schedule had been debilitating. 'We were there for hours, I can't remember how many sessions we did. Musicians just kept coming in, listening to the mixes and enjoying our irreverent attitude to the whole thing.' The results were amazing – there can't be many artists in their dotage who'd have the nerve to tackle the Doors' 'Roadhouse Blues', but Rolf did a winning take on the old Jim Morrison song. His rendering of two hoary old Stones numbers, '(I Can't Get No) Satisfaction' and 'Honky Tonk Women', were equally thrilling – almost as subversive in their way as the Splodgenessabounds and John Otway takes of 'Two Little Boys' had been.

The deconstruction of Lou Reed's famed sexually ambiguous 1972 hit, 'Walk On The Wild Side' was mindblowing, with the girl backing singers adding a great 'doo-de-doo, de-doo-didgeridoo' that mocked the original's background chorus. For 'Great Balls Of Fire', Rolf himself added the vamping keyboard at the start of the song that recalled Jerry Lee Lewis's own pounding, percussive style. 'I did the piano,' he told *Goldmine*. 'I've been playing since I was nine. Just that boogie, then the band took over.'

'Bad Moon Rising', the old Creedence Clearwater Revival hit, that had been so chillingly used in Jon Landis's ace movie *An American Werewolf In London*, had so much of it original swamp voodoo removed from it that it sounded like a Eurovision Song Contest entry, while Rolf joined in the Troggs revival already under way thanks to Wet Wet Wet and their chart-topping 'Love Is All Around' to turn 'Wild Thing' (actually written by Chip Taylor) into a lilting Jamaican-style jaunt.

The album's undoubted highlight was a rendition of Deep Purple's 1972 hit, 'Smoke On The Water', originally recorded for the heavy metal band's 'Machine Head' set, and regarded as another hard-rocking *tour de force*. The song had been inspired by a fire in the studio where they wanted to cut the album and so it had been actually recorded on a mobile studio in the corridor of a Swiss hotel – but the way Rolf performed turned the lyrics into almost gobbledegook, a flat piano figure replacing the scorching guitar riff of the original.

The album was rounded out by the inclusion of 'Stairway' and three Rolf evergreens, 'Two Little Boys', 'Jake The Peg' and 'Tie Me Kangaroo Down Sport'. No sooner had the album been unleashed than Rolf was immediately out on the college circuit, promoting it on the college circuit. 'The magic of entertaining,' he wrote in *The Guardian*, 'is actually speaking to individuals in the audience, and if you don't learn that lesson, you never achieve your potential. It takes courage, but you've got to meet their eyes. If you tell jokes to the floor or wall, two thirds of the audience will be thinking about their next dental appointment. If you talk to one person sincerely, everybody thinks you're talking to them personally.'

And Rolf's musical endeavours didn't end there. He somehow managed to find time to learn the bagpipes – an incredibly difficult instrument to master – to appear at the Edinburgh Festival that summer in full Scots traditional dress (kilt and all) to lead a parade of 300 pipers and drummers from different parts of the world into the city as part of a charity campaign being organised by the Marie Curie cancer research fund. It was the biggest event of its kind.

Meanwhile, *Animal Hospital* took a rest over the summer, and ITV screened another series, *Cat Crazy*, which featured Rolf interviewing various celebrities and their pet felines. And he was among cats of a larger, more ferocious kind for a new series, *Zoo Watch Live*, from London Zoo that the BBC broadcast in the autumn, as well as an eagerly anticipated third run of *Animal Hospital*.

The show was now so successful that the BBC even released a video of some of the highlights of the first two series. Rolf was featured checking up on the recovery of some of the animals that had caught the public's imagination like Benji the dog who recovered after a life-saving operation, Bart the iguana who had to be held down with masking tape for an X-Ray to be carried out and Brandy the frisky feline who turned the surgery upside down. Co-presenter Steve Knight was seen on some of the series' most exciting emergency calls such as the rescue of an ape imprisoned in a garden shed for two years. Each video sale earned a royalty for the overworked, understaffed RSPCA hospitals around the country.

Rolf, reprising his role of Baron Hardup in *Cinderella* at the Hippodrome Theatre in Birmingham, also found time to rustle up his own inimitable brand of Christmas cheer. In November he released a new single through Ris Records. Entitled 'Ego Sum Pauper', the song, explained Rolf, 'means "I am poor" and the proceeds will go to Children In Need. I've never been much of a classicist, but it's a Latin song which I picked up in the 1960s and have always carried it in my head.' It wasn't a hit, but perhaps it was the sentiments that mattered.

The year of 1996 was a time of consolidation rather than another wave of the amazing highs that had characterised much of Rolf's career during the century's final decade. He introduced a run of programmes for the Beeb, *Animal Hospital Heroes*, which was in effect a compilation of highlights from past series. And in May there was a new programme on the air which crossed the Hospital series with Zoo Watch entitled *Animal Hospital On The Hoof*, which was broadcast from Whipsnade Wild Animal Park in Bedfordshire. And a new series of the ever-popular *Animal Hospital*, as ever transmitted live from North London, was screened in the autumn. Once again, it won the Most Popular Factual Entertainment Show at the second National TV Awards that October.

For much of 1996 Rolf was on the road and he had a new record to promote. In May, Living Beat Records released his version of the Queen rock classic 'Bohemian Rhapsody'. The original song had been a Number 1 hit for the 'Cecil B de Mille of rock'n'roll' over the Christmas period 1975 – a mock mini-opera with some of the most ambitious vocal arrangements ever incorporated into a pop song. In his own inimitable way, Rolf totally re-arranged it and deflated it of all its original self-importance. Unfortunately it failed to emulate the chart success accorded Freddie Mercury and company's original.

Meanwhile the live work kept rolling in: in October he topped the bill on the final night of the three-week Holsten Pils Beer Festival. The marquee was brimming over with a crowd who'd obviously all partaken of too much of the old amber nectar, but it didn't stop the teetotal Rolf from pulling out all the stops. He ran through his usual repertoire of favourites to roars of drunken approval and his language was surprisingly 'choice' which made his set go down even better – perhaps this 'not in front of the children' act was X-rated Rolf for the mums and dads!

But it was the kids who were first in mind when Christmas came around. Rolf once again took on the role of Baron Hardup in *Cinderella*, this time at the New Victoria Theatre in Woking in the company of Gary Wilmot, Robin Cousins, Judy Cornwell, Bob Carolgees and Spit the Dog. Reviewing the show, *The Surrey Advertiser* wrote, 'Gary (Wilmot) makes it look easy. Two shows a day and he still makes us feel that he's having a good time and loving every minute. So too does Rolf Harris who plays Baron Hardup, Cinders' Dad. Jake the Peg must be drawing his pension by now, but he still manages to delight audiences.'

Capitalising on his fame as a friend of all creatures great and small, Rolf illustrated and co-authored a new book with Mark Leigh and Mike Lepine. Entitled *True Animal Tales*, the book compiled Rolf's favourite animal stories from around the world. Gathering these shaggy dog stories (and more) into thematic groups such as 'Batty Beasts' and 'Feathered Friends', it was a perfect Christmas present chock full of delightful real-life anecdotes that ranged from the hilarious to the heart-warming.

There was the tale of the baboons at a safari park who used a banana to lure an unsuspecting antelope to stand by their enclosure wall so that they could leap on its back and vault to freedom. And there was the story of Daisy the Friesian cow who was separated from her calf, sent to market and sold to another farmer. The cow escaped and set off back six miles across country to be with her baby. There were brave pigs, painting elephants and a chimp who escaped from London Zoo on a double-decker bus! So potent was its animal magic that the tome became an instant Number 1 festive bestseller.

Animals were still Number 1 for Rolf in early 1997 as, on 20 March, he embarked on a brand new series of *Animal Hospital*. This latest helping of Casualty animal-style broke with tradition and found itself a new operating base – the Hampden Veterinary Hospital in Aylesbury, a practice that had been going for more than 60 years. The only familiar faces were those of Steve Knight, Shauna Lowry (who replaced original presenter Lynda Bryans) and, of course, good old Rolf. Not only was there a new group of vets and nurses to meet but the new series expanded its horizons by visiting the Equine Hospital at Shorndown.

Viewers were also taken to a local farm to catch up on the lambing and calving, there were puppy socialisation classes, even check-ups on the health of exotic birds in a local aviary. Said Colin Price, head of the Small Animal Practice at Hampden, 'It's a terrifying prospect, but people tell me we won't notice the cameras after a couple of days! I know we've got a hard act to follow, but we're looking forward to the challenge. There's a balance sheet with fun on one side and stress on the other. So long as the fun outweighs the stress, it will be great.'

Talking of the latest series, Shauna Lowry observed: 'It's lovely, there's such a great atmosphere, the locals are really excited about us being at Aylesbury. I like to muck in and get my hands dirty. I'll be out and about with the farm vets and hopefully be at the birth of a foal. The vets cover up to 200 miles a day and I will be accompanying them on their visits and helping out at the hospital', while Steve Knight commented, 'you never know what the day will bring. I'm really looking forward to the lambing season and hopefully I'll get the chance to help out. We all like to get involved when we can – only the other day I was feeding baby ostriches!'

Rolf was as enthusiastic as ever. 'The best bit is meeting the real people. I love the fact that it isn't scripted and that you just talk to them as you would in real life and go with your emotions. Often they're very tense and anxious about their animal, and I'm a face they've known all their life from TV, so it's like having an old friend there. People feel they can trust me, so my role is very satisfying. I can comfort them, and their pet, and also ask the vet the kind of of questions they're often too nervous to ask.

'My role is a demystifying one – if the vet talks about the anterior bone, or something, I can say "what's that?". It takes a lot of pressure off them.' With viewing figures still well over the 11 million mark, the nation gave the new cast and crew an overwhelming vote of confidence.

July saw Rolf fronting a second series of *Cat Crazy* for ITV as well as *Animal Hospital Revisited* in which the entertainer paid some return visits to Harmsworth Hospital to catch up on what had become of some of the most memorable patients from previous episodes. These included Ben the dog who'd been kept locked up in a cellar until he'd been rescued by RSPCA inspectors, and the tiny kitten that had been found left in a toilet to drown. Viewers were also delighted that the two 'water-logged' ducks that had caused so much concern had finally found a home with presenter Steve Knight and his family. Rolf followed this by another tour down under.

And at the ripe old age of 67, there is no sign of him slowing down. The autumn will see yet another run of *Animal Hospital* and the release of a new album along the lines of *'Rolf Rules OK'* that saw him return to his long-time record label EMI. Titled *'Can You Tell What It Is Yet?'*, this was again a collection of contemporary songs. Among the tracks tackled were Lou Reed's 'Perfect Day' (emulating the success of his earlier 'Walk On The Wild Side') and 'Hand In My Pocket' from grunge goddess Alanis Morissette.

In keeping with its title, the album cover cleverly showed just a small bit of Rolf's illustration: the cover had to be opened out to get the full effect. Best of all, there was a limited edition bonus disc of children's songs, performed in inimitable Rolf Harris fashion, for his younger fans to enjoy.

One more musical project remained as yet unfulfilled. In the late 1980s he covered 'Raining On The Rock' by leading Aussie country and western singer John Williamson. Perhaps one day Rolf would return to his Australian roots and record material by some his home country's acts. The idea of Harris 'interpreting' songs by the likes of eco-activists Midnight Oil is positively intriguing, as is the concept of duets with the likes of Nick Cave or even Kylie Minogue!

EPILOGUE

The man is simply unstoppable. 'When one door closes another opens, if you're lucky. And if you're ready to jump, there are always chances', he told *Radio Times:* 'My career has been amazing. Every now and again it seems to come up with something different. I find it staggering...every successful record I've had has been a complete left turn from the last.'

Rolf Harris, OBE, Member of the Order of Australia and all-round entertainer, is a national institution on two continents – to use one of his favourite expressions, his life has been 'bloody marvellous.' It looks almost certain that there may yet be one or two doors left for him to open.